Unders

Songs in Renewal

Victoria Cooke

GROVE BOOKS LIMITED
RIDLEY HALL RD CAMBRIDGE CB3 9HU

Contents

The Cover Illustration is by Peter Ashton

First Impression April 2001
ISSN 1470-8531
ISBN 1 85174 462 2

1

When a Song is More Than a Song

The Charismatic Movement has been an increasingly influential part of the experience of the wider church for over thirty years. With many charismatics in traditional denominations as well as the emerging churches of the 'House Church' movement, the Charismatic Movement 'boasts more than 20 million adherents and has significantly touched the entire world.'[1] One of the most recognizable and distinctive features of the Charismatic Movement is its 'new hymnody'—the use of music and song in worship. The popularity of this new style of worship has grown to the point where there can be 'few Anglican churches who have not encountered the music of the renewal movement.'[2] The new hymnody has become over time a cross-denominational phenomenon.

In common with other Christians, charismatics are concerned that the whole of life be lived in a way honouring to God. But for charismatics worship is focussed in the act of coming together as God's people to praise, honour and respond to God through music and song. Thus, charismatic worship usually includes a time of extended 'worship' where several songs are sung back to back as part of the church service. The same format is evident at charismatic gatherings of all sizes from personal prayer and house groups to conferences and conventions. Worship does not end with the final chord of a song. But for charismatics the worship service vitalizes and shapes the life of worship in which the whole of the self is offered to the glory and service of God.

Songs are theological carriers of the highest calibre—but they are not always carriers of first rate theology. The emotional, aesthetic and affective dimensions of joyful song means that, for good or ill, the theology a song carries quickly finds its way into the minds and hearts of those who sing it. Often songs are selected not for reasons of theological appropriateness but for reasons of popularity verging on faddishness. But the very fact that most members of a congregation cringe at some aspect of one new song or another is an invitation to engage in deeper theological reflection on the themes of worship songs. For those responsible for the leading worship such reflection is an urgent pastoral responsibility.

Whatever the merits or otherwise of the music of these songs, our focus will be on the theological content of charismatic worship songs. This is not to deny the importance of other factors but is merely to concentrate on the primary way they influence and shape the life and mission of the church. In what follows I will introduce the main theological themes of three popular and influential charismatic schools of song writing. I will then draw together some of the main theological themes and consider the practical implications for worship and worshippers.

---

1   J I Packer, *Keep in Step with the Spirit* (Leicester: Inter-Varsity Press, 1984) p 170.
2   J Begbie, 'The Spirituality of Renewal Music: A Preliminary Exploration,' *Anvil*, Vol 8, No 3, 1991, p 227.

2
Charismatic Worship Songs—A Description

What makes a song identifiable as 'charismatic'? In his 1991 article, Jeremy Begbie described the main themes of charismatic worship songs in six groups: (a) songs of exuberant praise; (b) songs of jubilant testimony and exhortation; (c) songs of intimacy with God; (d) songs of majesty; (e) songs of hushed reverence; and (f) songs of battle. Whilst not comprehensive, Begbie's summary provides us with a helpful starting point.[3] Since 1991, however, there have been significant developments in the predominant trends of worship—so much so that I believe it is now necessary to re-categorize the main worship themes in charismatic hymnody. Thus I have chosen the following five categories:

1) *Songs of Praise:* This is one of Begbie's original categories, and refers to songs which are typically up-tempo and addressed directly to God or Jesus.

2) *Songs of Love and Commitment*: Begbie wrote of simple intimate love songs, sung directly to the Father/Jesus/God, which often say little more than 'I love you.' Now, however, there are more songs of love *and* commitment. Few songs stop simply at 'I love you'; most go on to say 'and I give my life to you.' Whilst not uncommon before, such songs are now just as frequent as simple love songs. To love God is to surrender everything to his purposes. Nothing but total commitment will do and it is each Christian's responsibility to recognize their role in the pursuit of such perfection.

3) *Songs of Intercession*: In the 60s and 70s it was more usual to speak of songs of warfare, that is, songs which declared the victory of the kingdom of God over all other powers. These, however, are less widely used in the contemporary church. More usual are songs which proclaim a confidence in God's ability to change lives and overcome difficulties. These are accompanied by songs of intercession which ask that God would answer the prayers of his people.

4) *Songs of Ministry:* These fall into two categories. Some songs are written to be sung to a congregation rather than by a congregation. Their main focus is on persuading listeners to be open to God and be honest about their emotions, problems and so on. They often encourage people to receive prayer ministry. On the other hand, some songs simply focus on God's attributes and the worshipper's relationship to him so as to draw the believer into an intimate relationship which is expected to enable healing to occur.

5) *Songs of Awe and Glory:* Begbie originally spoke of songs of intimacy, majesty and awe. Some of these songs are now covered by my category of love and commitment. Others simply and specifically focus on the glory of God. Such songs affirm God's nearness to his people and are a result of, and a petition for, an intense encounter with God.

---

3   Jeremy Begbie, 'The Spirituality of Renewal Music,' p 231.

Any particular song will not always fit into only one category and may even change categories depending on the context and way in which it is used. These five categories are only meant as an indication of the major themes reflected in the content of the songs and an indication of the ways in which they are often used. Such categories are neither exhaustive nor do they account for everything that is out there in a rapidly changing movement. During the course of the next few chapters I will use these descriptive categories to explore the theology of three of the most popular worship song-writing schools of the present time and point out any distinctive kinds of songs which do not fit into the above summary.

3

Matt Redman

By 1994, Matt Redman had been thrust into the arena of Renewal worship through leading worship at the 'Soul Survivor' and 'New Wine' conferences.[4] Since then, he has produced numerous worship albums and attracts large numbers wherever he is invited to lead worship.

Redman's songs have displayed a distinct shift of emphasis through time. Whilst the themes of praise and commitment can both be found throughout Redman's work, the emphasis, indicated by syntax, number and selection of songs used in worship events, has shifted from praise to commitment. Many early Redman songs focused upon praise, thanksgiving, the wonder of the cross and the gift of salvation. Whilst this element remains in his later work, during the last few years Redman's talent for writing about commitment and personal sacrifice have come to the fore. Such development is not unexpected as Redman's theology has developed since becoming a worship leader in the early nineties at a very young age.

The Cross Has Said It All

The cross is a recurrent theme, not only in Redman's more reflective songs, but also in his songs of praise. *The Cross Has Said It All* is representative of Redman's early approach to the cross, where the main focus was on rejoicing in the gift of salvation. This is a lively song, and the tempo is meant to reflect the joy and confidence that comes from knowing the effects of the cross. The lyrics are almost a compendium of biblical quotations and imagery demonstrating God's love, the

---

4   The Soul Survivor conference is aimed at young people (14-20+). Through his prominent position here, Redman has become a lead figure in shaping the worship of the younger generation of worshippers in the UK. New Wine is the adult counterpart to Soul Survivor.

effect of the death of Christ and the human condition. The effect of the cross is summed up in the opening line and worked out in verse one:

> The cross has said it all, the cross has said it all.
> I can't deny what you have shown, the cross speaks of a God of love;
> there displayed for all to see, Jesus Christ, our only hope,
> a message of the Father's heart, 'Come, my children, come on home.'

The cross is a demonstration of the love of the Father's heart to the children he loves and therefore provides his own Son as the answer to humanity's most basic need. This love is immeasurable, but visible in the cross. As such, this song houses a model that has become a key way of looking at the cross in modern Renewal worship. With echoes of the parable of the Prodigal Son and close affinity with Abelard's understanding of the atonement as exemplary love, the cross is portrayed as the Father's heart, crying 'Come my children, come on home.' Redman's understanding is summed up perfectly in a song he later wrote for Soul Survivor 1998 called *Saved*, where the chorus ends with the climactic words: 'Jesus this is how I know what love is, you died for me.'

A Response to the Cross

While the cross remains a source of joy and praise, it was also to form the basis for Redman's approach to a response of love. *Jesus Christ (Once Again)*, was one of Redman's songs which was to find a lasting place in many charismatic worship services, especially in association with Communion services. Here, the worshipper is invited to consider the cross and make a humble response to the gift of love which it reveals. Written in the same year as *The Cross Has Said It All*, *Jesus Christ* focuses on the sacrifice of Jesus. The cross is the place where Jesus 'became nothing' and was 'poured out to death.'

The real heart of this song is the way in which Redman draws the worshipper from focusing on the sacrifice of Christ, to make a link between this and the worshipper making a response to this sacrifice. The response elicited is mainly that of praise and wonder: 'But for now I marvel at this saving grace and I'm full of praise again.' But this is accompanied by a hint of something more—'once again I pour out my life.' This emphasis on offering a response of more than 'thank you' is to be found again and again in Redman's songs.

Awe and Love

These are the two main responses found throughout Redman's work. Awe and wonder at the gift of the cross are usually found connected with an intimate relationship between Christ and the worshipper, so that praise and worship takes on a very personal feel. Such worship is often expressed through simple and repetitive songs in which the words are intended as a vehicle for a much deeper expression of thanks on the part of each and every worshipper. Examples of such songs include: *Friend of Sinners, I Have Come to Love You* and *Now Unto the King*.

Such songs are clear examples of 'Songs of Awe and Glory.' As such, they have relatively little theological content. The focus, rather, is on offering an expression of love to a God who has shown love through his Son.

One interesting development of this response to God, is that such intimacy becomes one of Redman's main desires in worship. Thus in *One Thing My Heart Is Set Upon* we hear: 'One thing my heart is set upon, one thing that I would ask; to know you, Lord, as close as one could hope to on this earth. Intimacy, O Jesus, intimacy. My treasure will be, O Jesus, your intimacy.'

Love and Commitment

The other response to the sacrifice of Christ is that of love and commitment. This finds its clearest expression in two of Redman's most popular and enduring songs: *I Will Offer Up My Life* and *When The Music Fades*. *I Will Offer Up My Life* is concerned with the worshipper's offering to God in return for the offering which Jesus made upon the cross. This is a song of commitment and recommitment, as the chorus makes clear:

> Saviour what can be said, what can be sung,
> as a praise of your name, for the things you have done?
> Oh my words could not tell, not even in part,
> for the debt of love that is owed
> by this thankful heart.

This debt of love involves the worshipper offering their whole lives, pouring it out as the 'oil of love,' an allusion to the act of worship of the woman who anointed Jesus' feet with perfume as a precursor to his crucifixion (John 12.1-11). Only such an act of total self-giving is a worthy response to the cross.

The sacrifice of Jesus is something that demands a great response, in fact the greatest possible human response. This is neatly encapsulated in one of Redman's most popular recent songs, *When The Music Fades*. Although no-one could ever repay Jesus, those who love him long to give him a worthy offering, not as a repayment, but as an expression of love and devotion to the 'king of endless worth.' Here, Redman expresses that his heart's desire is to respond to Jesus with 'more than a song,' for Jesus searches the heart of the worshipper for 'something that's of worth.' The only offering worth offering is everything: 'Though I'm weak and poor, all I have is yours, every single breath.'

Reaching out to the 'Lost'

Another theme that has become increasingly central to the worship songs of Redman is the notion that commitment to evangelism is a central response to be offered in worship. Even in Redman's early songs, there is clearly a desire that the lost should be saved. *It's Rising Up* makes the petition: 'Oh let the cry to nations ring that all may come and all may sing,' while *We've Had A Light* encourages worshippers to 'take the truth, whatever the cost,' since the blessing of salvation 'carries a challenge to go.'

Songs from 1997 onwards, however, displayed a much clearer focus on the pursuit of 'Revival' and with it came an upsurge in songs of intercession. Matt Redman's albums from the 1997 and 1998 Soul Survivor conferences are evidence of this. The 1997 album contains a song which declares that each worshipper will be 'a history maker...a speaker of truth to all mankind' and 1998 saw the release of the song *Can A Nation Be Changed* which asked that the nation be turned back to God. Such songs were accompanied by teaching on the importance of evangelism, using the teaching of Christ and the examples of the early church. Many such services would end with a call to increased commitment to saving the lost.

It is easy to see why such teaching became dominant in the Soul Survivor stream. Designed as a vehicle to reach and enthuse young people, converts are usually young and bring with them the enthusiasm of youth. Soul Survivor needs only to fire such enthusiasm and back it with good solid teaching in order to equip and empower worshippers to take the gospel to their friends and families. Such an approach was then later fed back into the New Wine conference (the adult version of Soul Survivor) and so came to become a characteristic of this strand of charismatic worship.

Conclusion

Matt Redman is possibly the most popular and widely used worship songwriter in the UK at the current time. He uses biblical material and allusions as the basis for many of his songs. The cross is a central theme in his music. He also takes seriously both Christian discipleship and mission, though on each of these themes his work could be criticized for lacking a breadth and depth of theological vision. Redman's focus is necessarily on facilitating engagement with God in worship and motivating for Christian service. In a generation afraid of commitment these are invaluable gifts to place at the service of the church.[5]

---

5   On the question of commitment and youth discipleship see further Graham Cray's *Postmodern Culture and Youth Discipleship* (Grove Pastoral booklet P 76).

4

The UK Vineyard Movement

The Vineyard Movement is a group in which it is quite easy to trace the development between the formularized theology and the worship songs which spring from that theology. Founded by John Wimber, the Vineyard Movement has its roots firmly set in the USA. The US has historically been the focal point for both the theology and the songs of the movement. In the last few years, however, there has been a surge in the output of worship songs from the UK Vineyard, resulting in the release of three albums of UK worship songs since 1998: *Come, Now Is The Time*, *Hungry* and *Surrender*.

All songs on these albums are written by various worship leaders from across the UK Vineyard network. As with the music of Matt Redman, there are certain themes which are recurrent in the Vineyard style of worship. Perhaps here, even more than for the Soul Survivor conferences, the songs define and reflect the theological roots from which these songs stem.

The Father Heart of God

An understanding of the importance of the love of God for his children is central if we are to appreciate Vineyard Worship music. I have taken the phrase 'The Father Heart of God' straight from the worship albums of the Vineyard Movement itself,[6] which is a clear demonstration of the importance of this notion in Vineyard theology. The 'Father Heart of God' was one of John Wimber's main theological concerns in his teaching. It was of prime concern to Wimber that worshippers both understood and experienced the love of God as a father rather than as a dictator, bully or tyrant. This aspect was therefore central to his teaching and subsequently of prime importance to the themes of Vineyard worship and forms a vital part of the Vineyard contribution to songs of ministry.

In UK Vineyard worship this strand has two main focal points. It is a combination of an emphasis on the fatherly nature of God and the intimate relationship between the Father and his children that forms the basis of the intimacy which exists in Vineyard worship, especially in songs of love, but also songs of praise and awe.

There are many examples within UK Vineyard worship that emphasize the fatherly aspects of God, and where the love of God is asserted and celebrated. *Hungry*, for example, affirms the worshipper's confidence that God's 'Arms are open wide.' *The Lord is Gracious* speaks of God as 'Slow to anger and rich in love' and that God has 'compassion for all that he has made' and therefore responds to the needs of those who seek him.

---

6   The Vineyard Movement produces albums of songs which seek to demonstrate the love of God and his Father-like care for his children under the umbrella title of 'The Father Heart of God.'

A Child of God

The second integral aspect of this emphasis on the 'Father heart of God' is the corresponding standing of worshippers. They should be confident that God draws each worshipper to him as a child of God: 'This is who I'm meant to be, I know you have chosen me' says the song *With You*. *When You Call My Name* addresses God and declares that '…you call my name [and] speak your confirmation.' The song *Child of God* from the *Hungry* album expresses this theology perfectly:

> Father you're all I need, my soul's sufficiency,
> my strength when I am weak, the love that carries me.
> Your arms enfold me, till I am only a child of God.

In some songs this analogy is extended to seeing the worshipper as a child, who is dependent upon God the Father just as a baby is dependent upon its mother. Such a resemblance can be clearly seen in the second album, *Hungry*, which uses as its cover picture a photograph of a baby looking upwards, presumably towards its mother. In other songs, such a relationship between God and the worshipper manifests itself in the worshipper seeing God as a place of rest and a shelter from the 'storms' of life. *What a Child Is Meant To Be*, for example, speaks of how worshippers should see themselves in relation to their Father God:

> In my weakness I find that your strength knows no bounds…
> and even with this fragile heart, I find a place to rest here,
> > safe where you are…
> Lord I'm learning that your love can cover me,
> you are teaching me what a child is meant to be.

Healing

Finding rest in the knowledge of God as a Father extends to become the basis of the Vineyard theology of healing. Moreover, for John Wimber, the ultimate sign that the kingdom of God is present is that of 'signs and wonders.' This was to become the cornerstone of Vineyard theology, especially in relation to evangelism and ministry. It is argued that in line with the model of the New Testament, God desires to minister to both believers and non-believers as a sign of his presence. This means that both Christians and non-Christians alike should expect to encounter the gifts of tongues, prophecy, interpretation and healing.

This strand of theology has naturally come to find expression in Vineyard worship albeit with a subtle alteration. While Wimber focused upon physical healing, worship songs tend to focus upon psychological healing. Wherever the ability of God to heal is proclaimed in song, it is accompanied by an affirmation of the frailty and weakness of human beings and their need for God's intervention in order to be made whole. Thus *Hungry* declares: 'Hungry I come to you…I am empty…broken I run to you…I am weary,' while *Refuge In You* declares God as being 'a hiding place' where worshippers can tell God all their troubles. All those who are thirsty are encouraged to come and 'let the pain and sorrow be washed away' by the waves of God's mercy.

It should not, however, be assumed that such affirmations are always solemn or grave. On the contrary, the Father's ability to heal the wounds of his children is something to be celebrated. It forms the heart of much of the praise to be found in the Vineyard songs. Thus, *Your Name Is Holy* declares: 'In your name there is strength to remain to stand in spite of pain.' *Who Is This* asks in wonder 'Who is this that wipes the tears from my eyes?' and declares: 'Just one glimpse of you steals my heart away.'

In chapter two I explained that there are two distinct kinds of songs of ministry and healing, that is songs sung *by* a congregation and songs sung *to* a congregation. In UK Vineyard worship we find clear expressions of the former of these two approaches. Songs which focus upon the fatherly characteristics of God both increase faith in God's desire to heal and also place an active responsibility on worshippers to acknowledge and proclaim in faith the relationship they have with God. The American Vineyard strand, however, contains more examples of ministry songs designed to be sung to a congregation, which may be connected with the phenomenon of the 'Toronto Blessing' although such influence would no doubt have been felt in the UK as well as in America. In practice, however, it is usual to find a variety of both styles of ministry songs used in worship.

Surrender

As with Redman, the theme of surrender is a key aspect of Vineyard theology—so much so that this one word is used for the title of the third album. Of the 38 songs on the three UK albums, 13 are clearly intended as songs of surrender, and others could be used as such. Of these 13 songs, the main emphasis is clear, as here in *Surrender*. The desires of the worshipper are to be surrendered to God:

> I'm giving you my heart and all that is within,
> I lay it all down for the sake of You my King.
> I'm giving you my dreams, I'm laying down my rights,
> I'm giving up my pride, for the promise of new life.

Such surrender is Vineyard's equivalent of Redman's theology of worship. Commitment to God involves the complete surrender of everything. It is easy to locate a biblical basis for this in Jesus' Gethsemane prayer 'not my will, but yours' (Luke 22.42) and Paul's exhortation that 'those who live should no longer live for themselves but for him who died for them and was raised again' (2 Cor 5.15).

A central aspect of such self-surrender is the pursuit of holiness. God is a holy God and those who seek him must also seek his holiness for if worshippers are to bring 'an offering of a consecrated life,' they must also sing: 'Over every thought, over every word, may my life reflect the beauty of my Lord.' Again this theme of holiness has clear echoes of Scripture, with Paul urging the churches time and again to be holy and live a life worthy of their calling.

Praise

The final element which is strong in the songs of the UK Vineyard Movement is that of praise. Vineyard songs delight in praising God and thanking him for all he is and all he has done. Especially prevalent in this strand is praise for the beauty of creation and the use of imagery taken from the Psalms. More often than not, praise is accompanied by an upbeat tempo and joyous, party-like feel. Songs tend to offer a confirmation of an attribute of God followed by a response of joy and delight, as in *Your Love is Amazing*:

> Your love is amazing, steady and unchanging,
> your love is a mountain, firm beneath my feet…
> hallelujah, hallelujah, hallelujah,
> your love makes me sing.

Conclusion

The distinctive Vineyard contribution to charismatic worship can be found in the expression of the relationship between the worshipper and God the Father, and the outworking of this relationship through healing and prayer ministry. There are obvious connections between the worship songs of the Vineyard Movement and those of Matt Redman, especially in relation to the theme of surrender. Vineyard arguably offers a more emotional version of the same themes that are found in Redman. This may be a consequence of the American roots of Vineyard worship. It is more likely, however, that this emotional element stems from the pervasive Vineyard theology of the Father heart of God, which continually encourages Christians to be emotional about their relationship with God just as they would be in any other healthy relationship. This is the fundamental characteristic of the Vineyard worship community and a major reason why such worship continues to make a significant contribution to the worship life of charismatics across the world.

5
Hillsongs, Australia

In 1993, Darlene Zschech released a song which was to quickly find its way into the worship lives of thousands of churches across the world. Several years later, *My Jesus, My Saviour* remains a firm favourite in the UK, often used week in and week out in all kinds of worship gatherings.

The success of *My Jesus, My Saviour* meant that charismatics from around the world became interested in the songs which were being produced in large quantities by the Australian Hillsongs writers. Consequently more of the songs from this school are now finding their way into charismatic congregations.

One of the most distinctive features of Hillsongs' worship publications is that often songs are accompanied by an explanation from the composers of the reasons for the writing of that particular song.[7] These short commentaries often give a key insight into the theological sources which have influenced Hillsongs' song writers. Many of these explanations point to specific biblical passages as the basic inspiration of a song. Others explain some of the theological trends which Hillsongs builds its worship upon and it is this which is of most interest to us. To illustrate this point, I will refer, where appropriate, to these 'commentaries' as I highlight the main elements of Hillsongs worship.

Celebration and Praise

Hillsongs give praise a prominent place, devoting a high proportion of songs to joy, celebration and upbeat praise. In all cases, these songs exude confidence in the love of God for his church, his love of the worship of the church and God's omnipotence in all things. It is difficult not to sense the pride with which these songs are meant to be sung—that is, the pride with which the worshipper sings about their God:

> When I am weak you make me strong,
> when I'm poor I know I'm rich,
> for in the power of your name,
> all things are possible.

The narrative accompanying this song, *All Things Are Possible*, characterizes such confidence as faith and makes a significant and unambiguous link between praise and faith: 'Praise releases faith. It's a fact.' The line of reasoning here is that to sing so confidently about the omnipotence of God cannot but increase the worshipper's 'level' of faith. If this is so, then this places an enormous responsibility upon composers to ensure that they do not raise the expectations of the worshipper

---

7   Such explanations can be found printed in the inlay cards of Hillsongs' CD publications.

beyond that which is biblically reasonable to expect.

Elsewhere, to accompany the song *My Heart Sings Praises*, Russell Frager offers these words: 'There is something about words of praise. They seem to release something in us, perhaps because they bring our soul into agreement with our spirit. Our spirits are alive to God, ready at any time to worship, but often waiting for our minds and emotions to catch up.' Whilst this is not, perhaps, the most eloquent of explanations, Fragar's point is clear—songs of praise should form an essential element of worship since they provide the external element which enables the soul to express its love for the creator. That the soul should and wants to worship God finds its home in the psalms where 'deep calls to deep' (Ps 42.7). It is reasonable logic to see songs of praise as a means to such an end.

Lives Changed by Christ

In terms of theological content, the distinctive feature of Hillsongs worship is the emphasis on celebrating lives that have been changed by meeting Jesus. While Redman and Vineyard place primary focus upon the worshipper's responsibility after conversion, Hillsongs seeks to celebrate the actual fact of conversion and the wonder of the work of Christ.

Conversion for Hillsongs creates an enormous sense of security in the love of God. Tanya Riches, commenting on her song *Jesus, What a Beautiful Name*, writes: 'No matter where I go, or what circumstances I face, no matter what I lose or what is taken from me, nothing can separate me from the love of God.' This theology has produced some of the most poetic songs of all three of my chosen Charismatic worship strands. This sense of security can be felt in *My Jesus, my Saviour* but also forms the heart of many other songs including *And that my soul knows very well, Jesus, What A Beautiful Name, My Heart Sings Praises* and *Thank You, Lord*.

It is interesting to note that in many respects such songs serve the same purpose as the Vineyard ministry songs in that they seek to reaffirm the relationship between God and the worshipper and in doing so depict God as a loving and caring protector of his children. The fact that this reaffirmation most often takes the form of praise does not alter its effect.

To Know God More

This emphasis on conversion does not remove the need for Hillsong worshippers to 'know God more.' But what does this phrase, 'to know God more,' mean? On the one hand, it is to deepen one's faith in the love of God; on the other hand, it is to surrender more fully to the desires of God. Reuben Morgan explains: 'The heart of God is for us to be completely sold out to him. Our thoughts, passions and dreams (everything that makes us who we are) only have true life as they become his to shape and to mould. As we give our heart and soul to God we then walk to endless riches that are found in intimacy with him.' Thus in *Let the Peace of God Reign* the worshipper cries: 'Lord, my heart is set on you. Let me run the race of time, with your life enfolding mine...Oh Lord I hunger for more of you. Rise up within me, let me know your truth.'

My Jesus, My Saviour

Popularity dictates that some mention be made of this, the most famous song published by Hillsongs. What is it about this song that has made it such a lasting and popular worship song? There is no easy answer, but I would like to offer some suggestions.

Firstly, *My Jesus, My Saviour* is an easy song to sing, and, if transposed, not too difficult to play. This makes it instantly accessible to congregations. The tune is catchy and the song moves at an easy pace. These are qualities which we see again and again in many of the songs that have become most popular in charismatic worship since they play a large part in making charismatic worship as a whole easy to access and maintain even in the smallest of congregations. Apart from this, however, the music also superbly fits the feel of the song. The crescendo, which accompanies the beginning of the chorus, fits the triumphant mood of the lyrics, raising the spirit to meet the soul in worship. The final line of the chorus, 'nothing compares to the promise I have in you' can be quietened down and repeated to suit an atmosphere of awe in worship, which so often accompanies this song.

But there is much also to be said for its lyrical content. So far I have categorized songs by type—praise, surrender, thanks and so on. *My Jesus, My Saviour* defies such categorization. For a charismatic, there is in this song an element of all the essential elements of worship. *My Jesus, My Saviour* contains praise and wonder, a celebration of the love of God, a promise to love and serve God always, and a final element of awe. It is this combination which makes *My Jesus, My Saviour* a catalyst, moving worshippers from a place of praise to a place of worship and in my experience it is for this reason that worship leaders will choose to use this song over and over again.

Conclusion

The popularity and therefore influence of Hillsongs worship will continue to remain prominent for at least as long as *My Jesus, My Saviour* continues to be widely used. It is reassuring then to see that Hillsongs are concerned not only to produce worship songs but to educate worshippers by explaining the thinking behind their songs. This commentary allows users to think more deeply about what they are singing and encourages greater sensitivity in their use by worship leaders. This is the theme which I will discuss more in the following chapter which will focus upon some of the most distinctive elements of a charismatic theology of worship.

6
A Charismatic Way of Worship?

In chapter two I introduced five categories of charismatic worship songs—praise, love and commitment, awe and glory, intercession, and ministry—which I described as being representative of the main themes of charismatic worship songs. We have seen these categories illustrated in the songs of Matt Redman, Vineyard and Hillsongs. Since we noted considerable overlap of themes and ideas, it is natural to ask: Is there something which makes a song 'charismatic'? Or, to put it another way: is it possible to speak of a common charismatic theology in worship? If there is a charismatic theology for worship, then how do the categories of worship songs we have identified reflect this theology?

The Roots of Charismatic Songs
The sources on which charismatic worship songs draw has an important influence on both the stock of theological ideas that the songs utilise as well as the specific theological content of a song. In this respect the explanations given by the Hillsongs writers are very revealing and for practical purposes can be taken as representative of the sources of charismatic worship songs in other charismatic streams. There are three main sources of inspiration for worship songs:

1) Biblical material
2) Sermons, prophetic messages and 'words'
3) Experience of the presence of God.

Charismatic worship employs biblical material in a whole host of ways just as in other traditions. Sermons and prophetic messages given in charismatic circles and experiences of God are often used as a source of inspiration or represent particular ways of interpreting or applying biblical texts. These two approaches are difficult to quantify as they will usually be specific to the individual situation.

It is the last of these three sources of inspiration—the use of charismatic experience as a source—which is most problematic because of the difficulties surrounding the authentication and reproduction of experiences of God in worship. How should a person evaluate or appropriate another's experience of the presence of God? Can experience of God in the Holy Spirit be expressed, conveyed or reinvoked in song? Should such experiences be used to form songs which when sung, embody and express an experientially-based theology? What about the problem of portability—how easily can songs embodying such a theology be transported outside their charismatic origins? Do they not lose their meaning or significance in other contexts? Songs which are intensely personal (like Redman's *When the Music Fades*) or speak of having experienced the presence of God in any sensory way point up these difficulties particularly sharply. There is not space here to address these questions—and in fact they are not crucial to an understanding of the theology of charismatic worship. But is is important to recognise these diverse sources of charismatic song-writing.

To Start at the Beginning

Fundamental to understanding the theology of charismatic worship songs is the premise from which such worship begins. The heart of the charismatic movement is about God and who he is: 'God as the present God, the living, loving, empowering God who comes to meet his people,' and this distinctive understanding is seen most clearly in corporate worship.[8]

When charismatics gather to worship, there is the anticipation that they will meet with God:

> The desire to know God, to meet with him. This is the key to Spirit-filled worship of God. Without this desire to stand in his presence, worship becomes a fruitless experience…The most important fruit of worship is God's presence. This is the very heart of worship.[9]

Charismatics believe that through today's worship songs people are enabled to worship in 'spirit and truth,' in fulfilment of Jesus' words to the Samaritan woman in John 4.21–24: 'a time is coming when you will worship the Father neither on this mountain nor in Jerusalem.' The possibility of encountering God's presence is no longer bound spatially, but is to be found in the experience of worship, for this is where God is revealed by his Spirit as he really is.

Why is Worship Through Song so Important?

Charismatic worship lends itself to drawing a relationship between worship and the temple of the Old Testament. The connection is not so much concerned with the spatial element, but the understanding that the temple was the dwelling-place of God. It was where he revealed his glory. For charismatics, the presence of the Lord is 'in this place,' that is, where worshippers meet together.

In Jewish theology, the temple has always had supreme religious significance. Jerusalem was the city of God and the temple was the supreme dwelling-place of God on earth. In 1 Kings 8.6-11, after the Priests had placed the Ark of the Covenant in the Most Holy place within the temple, 'the cloud filled the temple of the Lord. And the priests could not perform their service, because of the cloud, for the glory of the Lord filled his temple' (1 Kings 8.10-11). This passage highlights three of the most important Jewish symbols for talking about the presence of God: the Ark, the cloud and glory. Of these three symbols, 'glory' has become a significant term in charismatic spirituality, as can be seen in one of Redman's later songs, *Lord, Let your Glory Fall*:

8   Russell, *Skepsis*, 'What is Happening When We Worship,' p 1.
9   Chris Bowater, *The Believer's Guide to Worship* (Eastbourne: Kingsway Publications, 1986) pp 20, 21.

Lord, let your glory fall, as on that ancient day.
Songs of enduring love, and then your glory came.
Your presence like a cloud, upon that ancient day.
The priests were overwhelmed, because your glory came.

The Glory of God

In the Old Testament, 'glory' is used as an attribute of God and is something that should be 'ascribe[d] to the Lord' (Ps 29.1). In the Old Testament, 'glory' is used to describe 'the manifest presence'[10] of God: (2 Chron 5.13-14; 1 Kings 8.10-13). Thus, 'while holiness expresses God's transcendence, his glory concerns rather his immanence to the world.'[11] The glory of the Lord is declared by the heavens (Ps 19.1), fills the whole earth (Num 14.21), and is to be proclaimed to all nations (1 Chron 16.24; Ps 96.3).

Glory was, however, most intensely experienced in the temple—so intense was the glory of the Lord in the temple on the day that the Priests placed the Ark in the Most Holy Place, that they could not perform their service (1 Kings 8.11). John Leach explains:

> The people [of Israel] would have been able to see when God was around because of what was described as a cloud, smoke or fire, filling the sanctuary …the smoke, like the flag flying on top of Buckingham Palace, was a sign that the King was in residence.[12]

To behold the glory of God is, for Bowater, the privilege of every Christian. If Moses, who was under the law, was able to see the glory of God, 'how much more should we who know Christ be able to come into his presence and "behold his glory."'[13]

Charismatic worship has readily adopted the idea that to speak of God's glory is to speak of his immanent presence[14] and it is this concept which leads to songs of awe and glory having such a prominent position within the repertoire of charismatic worship. Such songs either seek to reassure worshippers that the 'presence of God is here,' or speak of a desire for God to meet with his people in worship. The latter of these two ideas is a strong theme in the Vineyard worship songs from the US. Thus, *Draw Me Closer*[15] presents its petition, 'So that I might

---

10   Chris Bowater, *A Believer's Guide to Worship*, p 21.
11   Leopold Sabourin, 'Glory of God,' in Bruce M Metzger and Michael D Coogan (Eds), *The Oxford Companion to the Bible* (Oxford: Oxford University Press, 1993) p 254.
12   John Leach, *Living Liturgy* (Eastbourne: Kingsway Publications, 1997) p 12.
13   Chris Bowater, *A Believer's Guide*, p 25.
14   The presence of God is not limited only to corporate worship, since 'God is always present.' There is, however, something particular about corporate worship since, 'to make himself specifically seen and known' God has always had 'to appear somewhere.' God desires to meet with his people and 'especially enjoys the environment of praise' (Bowater, *A Believer's Guide*, pp 21-23).
15   Stuart Deavene and Glenn Gore, *Draw Me Close* (Mercy/Vineyard Publishing/Music Services/Copycare, 1987).

see you…your glory and your love.' *Father of Creation*[16] asks God to let his 'glory fall in this room.' The Hillsongs song *Lord We Long To See Your Glory* opens with the words 'Lord we long to see your glory, to gaze upon your lovely face,' and later uses the petition 'let us stay in your presence.'

On the other hand, there many other songs which celebrate the closeness of God and make a response to God's presence. It is the presence of God which leads to a response of love and commitment, intimacy and a recognition of the responsibility of salvation—all of which have been important themes in the songs of Matt Redman, Vineyard and Hillsongs.

The Holy Spirit

The vital link between the presence of God and the environment of worship is the charismatic theology of the Holy Spirit. Charismatic worship is understood as being 'Spirit-filled worship' since intimacy—'meeting God' in worship—is impossible without the Holy Spirit. In his list of 'definitions of worship' Bob Sorge explains that worship is essentially 'God's Spirit within us contacting the Spirit in the Godhead.'[17] Sorge explains that 'spiritual worship is the exclusive privilege of those who have been quickened by the…Holy Spirit.'[18] In fact, so integral is this aspect of the work of the Holy Spirit that Sorge sees it as one of the fundamental reasons why Jesus gave the Spirit to the church. As such, while the Holy Spirit is referred to directly in some songs, the role of the Holy Spirit should be taken to be always present, if at times implicitly, in charismatic worship.

Healing Power

It is because the Holy Spirit inhabits worship that worship is expected to have a dramatic effect upon worshippers and hence the emphasis on ministry and intercession which we have seen thus far. Chris Bowater explains that the presence of God, wherever it is displayed, will always be 'evidential.'[19] Charismatic spirituality believes that worship—a meeting between God and his people—is an occasion for God's grace to be active amongst those who have come to worship him, hence the prominence of charismatic songs which speak of healing. The 'Cross of Jesus' leads to freedom from sin thereby allowing for the healing of 'the wrongs we have done and the wrongs done to us';[20] it is the Father who brings comfort, shelter and healing to those who come to worship him.[21] *Be Still* proclaims, 'He [God] comes to cleanse and heal, to minister his grace' whilst the chorus of *I Believe in Jesus* asserts:

16   David Ruis, *Father of Creation*, (Mercy/Vineyard Publishing/Music Services/Copycare, 1992).
17   Bob Sorge, *Exploring Worship* (New York: Bob Sorge Ministries, 1996) p 65.
18   Bob Sorge, *Exploring Worship*, p 77.
19   Chris Bowater, *A Believer's Guide*, p 23.
20   Graham Kendrick and Steve Thompson, *How can I be free from sin* (Make Way Music, 1991).
21   Brain Doerksen, *Father Me* (Mercy/Vineyard Publishing, 1994).

And I believe he's [Jesus] here now
Standing in our midst.
Here with the power to heal now
And the grace to forgive.[22]

Confidence in God

The focus on healing is accompanied by the general emphasis on the victory of Christ, over sin, death and hell.[23] This emphasis could mean that charismatics do not focus on the 'dark side' of faith. But in reality, charismatic songs reveal that issues such as pain, sin, repentance, intercession and the like do feature, but usually in a context of confidence in God's ability to overcome. Thus for Matt Redman to write in the title words to one of his songs *When I Needed A Saviour, You Were There* is to imply a need for healing. Further on in the same song, Redman speaks more explicitly and directly about God's loving intervention in various times of need. Thus the pre-chorus reads:

You made me fruitful in the land of my suffering, Father.
You made me hopeful in the land of no hope;
poured oil of gladness on the wounds of my struggling…
poured oil of healing on the depths of my soul.

The tough themes of human existence are acknowledged. But they are also caught up in the conviction of the power of the living God to transform and heal.

A God Who Can Change The World

Such confidence in the Lord, and a focus on God's activity amongst his people in worship, also leads to an increased faith that God can intervene and change things occurring outside the church and in the lives of those who do not yet worship him. This is why intercession has an important place in charismatic worship, something which goes some way to counterbalancing claims that charismatic worship is indulgent and self-centred. Songs suggest, yet again, that it is the presence of the Holy Spirit which will make a difference in the world. Thus:

Lord we long for you to move in power.
There's a hunger deep within our hearts
to see healing, in our nation.
Send your Spirit to revive us.

Heal our nation!
Pour out your Spirit on this land![24]

---

22 Marc Nelson, *I believe in Jesus* (Mercy/Vineyard Publishing/Music Services/Copycare, 1987).
23 See Matt Redman, *The Cross Has Said It All*; *There's A Sound of Singing*.
24 Trish Morgan, *et al*, *Lord We Long for You* (Kingsway's Thankyou Music, 1986).

A Response of Praise

So far I have made no mention of praise, although it was the first of my five categories back in chapter two. Praise is probably one feature which always unites the individual strands of charismatic worship songs. We have already seen a number of examples from Matt Redman, Vineyard and Hillsongs in the previous chapters. For charismatics, the natural response to God's gift of salvation, promise of healing, and concern for the world is to praise him. To thank God for all of his gifts and celebrate the love of God has firm biblical roots. It draws especially on the Psalms and doxological material of the New Testament and is echoed in more traditional forms of worship across all denominations.

A Part of the Larger Picture

The popularity of songs from particular 'schools' of song-writing can make charismatic groups more vulnerable to the theological interests of a few narrow sources. The songs of Matt Redman, or indeed of any worship leader or song writer, are unlikely to provide a congregation with a broad, complete and healthy worship diet. In practice most charismatic song writers themselves rarely use only their own material in leading worship. Even when worship leaders choose large amounts of their own material this is usually supplemented with songs written by others, in order to provide more rounded worship. Both song writers and others responsible for the conduct of worship amongst charismatics commonly show considerable sensitivity to the need both for variety and for coherence in the selection and use of worship songs. Such intermixing dilutes both the strengths and weaknesses of each theological contribution.

Matt Redman, Vineyard and Hillsongs are not the only sources of worship songs used in charismatic worship across the UK. These three examples were chosen as examples of worship 'schools' which are having a significant impact upon contemporary charismatic worship. There are of course many other song-writers whose work is pervasive and whose theological themes both reproduce and complement those we have considered. Graham Kendrick, for example, places considerable emphasis on the incarnation and reflection upon the life, death and resurrection of Christ. Kendrick's songs also have a distinctive and keen emphasis upon social justice reflecting his involvement in the Ichthus churches of South East London. Others like David Fellingham, Stuart Townsend, and Paul Oakley write from within the more Calvinistically-inclined New Frontiers International group of New Churches. It is possible to detect in these a determination to set Scripture to music as well as a commitment to the revival of traditional hymnody for use within charismatic worship. Other popular writers include Noel Richards, Robin Mark, Chris Bowater, Trish Morgan, Jonny Markin, and David Townsend. In each case the productivity and creativity of such a range of writers ensures the provision of a diverse pool of material and an informal mechanism for quality control.

With the exception of some large worship 'concerts,' charismatic worship songs always form part of a larger act of worship, however complex or simple the rest of the service might be. Songs of intercession are an excellent example of the way in which many charismatic worship songs are intended for use within the wider context of a worship service. The most popular and enduring songs of intercession are those which offer a framework through which prayers of intercession for a range of situations can be offered. In other words, the words of a song are not meant to restrict or replace other aspects of worship (in this case intercessory prayers) but to accompany and facilitate them. Such songs are *both* words of worship in their own right *but also* vehicles for other forms of worship. Consequently intercession, confession, prayer for healing, concern for holy living and mission can all be supplemented rather than supplanted by wisely-used charismatic worship songs. When used in this way, the songs locate other aspects of worship within the theological framework I have outlined and help to direct that worshipping community into the specific form of direct devotional engagement with the living God.

Whilst there is hardly a theme of Christian theology not dealt with in some charismatic song or other, it remains the case that some themes still receive scant attention. By and large these cluster around the 'hard themes' of Christian living. For example, there are relatively few worship songs on the theme of confession. This is not to say that the confession of sin is not important in charismatic faith. There are popular songs which speak of the need for forgiveness and a recognition of sin—for example Gerrit Gustafson's *Only by Grace Can We Enter*. And songs of surrender can be used as a springboard for confession of times when God's will has not been of prime importance in the worshipper's life. So this theme may not be prominent within the charismatic repertoire but with careful thought it is possible to find songs which can be used within the context of confession. A bit of digging makes it possible to find worship songs for most everyday 'liturgical' contexts.

7
Getting the Best from Charismatic Songs

Despite its popularity, charismatic worship is subject to repeated criticisms. It is variously described as 'trivial,' 'theologically trite,' 'individualistic,' 'full of mindless repetition,' 'introspective,' 'manipulative,' 'full of unsavoury connotations.'[25] Others see such worship as far too much a human-centred rather than God-centred activity.[26] But much of the devotional power of charismatic worship songs derives from their memorability, familiarity, simplicity and flexibility. They help to shape and deepen the spiritual lives of thousands of believers from many different backgrounds and traditions. We have seen that these ecumenical, missiological and pastoral advantages need not be played off against educational potential and theological content. What can be done practically to get the most out of the best charismatic worship songs for today's churches? Here are five suggested priorities for those who want to exploit their potential.

Purposefulness. Thought needs to be given to the purpose for the selection and use of worship songs. Ultimately they are tools of pastoral care, facilitating the worship and edification of a congregation. It can help to set down on paper some simple reasons for using this kind of worship. Using such songs because they are popular or because young people like them appear to be valid justifications but are rather weak. Thinking through and making explicit the motivations for using this kind of vehicle for worship has a number of advantages. It will help all concerned to begin a path of theological reflection on what they are doing as they worship. It will help prevent charismatic worship taking on a life of its own and becoming an end in itself. And it will provide a check against which the need for renewal and change of patterns of worship can be judged.

Integration. Tolerance for the use of worship songs varies from place to place and service to service. Some worship concerts expect wall-to-wall singing. Most churches with a recognizably charismatic style use these songs as part, but only part, of their worship. Other churches may have less familiarity or tolerance for this style of song. But many want to move towards using them more or simply to using them as part of a more eclectic package. Providing a balanced diet of worship will be more or less exposed to strengths and weaknesses of the range of charismatic songs available depending on what part they are to play in an overall worship event. Here the key is integration—the sensible use of what these songs have to offer to complement the rest of a service. Simply using the songs as replacements for traditional hymns (stand up—sing once—sit down) is not to exploit their affective potential to the full. When there is a stronger liturgical structure the range of themes that need to be carried by charismatic songs can be allowed to narrow.

25 Jeremy Begbie, 'The Spirituality of Renewal Music,' p 227.
26 Tom Smail, Andrew Walker and Nigel Wright, *Charismatic Renewal* (SPCK: London, 1995) p 51.

Often those involved in leading a service will want the themes of the songs to inform the rest of worship. Thoughtfulness about the contribution of such worship songs can improve the coherence and vitality of an act of worship and can avoid leaving the sense that songs are 'bolted on' or 'taking over.'

Co-ordination. Both in the writing and use of charismatic songs there is more need for those who are musically inclined to co-operate with those who have theological insights to offer. The most enduring of contemporary songs combine creative excellence in music, poetry and theological insight. Well-led worship involves encouraging and expecting theological awareness of those responsible for leading worship. This means giving time and energy to opening and maintaining dialogue between preachers and worship leaders for the sake of mutual education, understanding and co-ordinated action.

Preparation. It is easy to get into a position where the range of available material for worship is determined by inappropriate factors, such as what is currently in vogue, or the preferences or capabilities of a music group leader. Good long-term preparation involves co-ordinated selection, learning and dissemination of a balanced range of material. The week before is too late to ask: 'What material could we use for Communion (intercession/confession)?' and reach for the least worst available option from the latest stock. Familiarity is an important feature of this charismatic hymnody but such availability can be nurtured with good long-term planning and preparation. A proactive policy of choosing material to learn and disseminate can ensure that theological merit can be given weight alongside other factors that influence the popularity of songs—such as a good tune or a famous writer.

Education. Charismatic worship songs are an educational tool in themselves. Leaders can exploit the strengths and ameliorate the weaknesses of the songs with good complementary education. This can be done in a number of formal and informal ways. Using songs to illustrate preaching is one common method. The continual use of songs to illustrate a systematic preaching series quickly reveals the dominant and absent themes in a church's current stock of worship resources. More directly, songs can be discussed in sermons on themes to which they relate. Where extempore prayers or other contributions are possible in worship a few well-placed comments, a prayer or Bible reading alongside a song can give a particular 'spin' that enhances or interprets its contents. In small groups like mid-week cell groups formal and informal (but gentle!) discussion of why a particular song is valuable, helpful, exciting or difficult in worship is a simple way of prompting worshippers to reflect on the theological and other merits of what they sing. By whatever means, the educational task of inviting the kind of thoughtfulness encouraged in simple form by the Hillsongs' 'commentaries' can enhance the discerning use of charismatic songs.

Used with these kinds of thoughtful considerations, charismatic worship songs can be powerful tools for the edification of the church.